DATE DUE			

BRIGHTER
BEGINNINGS
FOR
TEACHERS

BRIGHTER BEGINNINGS FOR TEACHERS

PATTY PULLEN

ScarecrowEducation
Lanham, Maryland • Toronto • Oxford
2004

Published in the United States of America
by ScarecrowEducation
An imprint of The Rowman & Littlefield Publishing Group, Inc.
4501 Forbes Boulevard, Suite 200, Lanham, Maryland 20706
www.scarecroweducation.com

PO Box 317
Oxford
OX2 9RU, UK

British Library Cataloguing in Publication Information Available

Library of Congress Cataloging-in-Publication Data

Pullen, Patty, 1938–
   Brighter beginnings for teachers / Patty Pullen.
      p. cm.
   Includes bibliographical references and index.
   ISBN 1-57886-095-4 (pbk. : alk. paper)
   1. First year teachers. I. Title.
   LB2844.1.N4 P85 2004
   371.1–dc22   2003024884

This book is lovingly dedicated to
The-World's-Finest-Husband,
and my favorite Ol' Dawg, Jim Kauffman,
without whom this book would still be an idea
running laps in my brain.

CONTENTS

PREFACE

The first day of my teaching career I bounced into my classroom with a big smile and a near-terminal case of naiveté. I was a speech pathologist without a lick of teaching experience, not even student teaching, but I was sure that teaching couldn't be too hard. So I smiled at my middle school students, who were milling around the room, and asked them to take a seat—whereupon the largest boy in the class grabbed a handful of my blouse, shook me, and said, "I'm gonna beat your honky ass!" My immediate thought was that there had to be an easier way to make a living.

I vividly remember my first year—all the horrors, the mistakes, and the trial and error that sometimes led to a maybe-I-can-do-this feeling, but more often to a what-made-me-think-I-could-do-this despair. That year, I searched the want ads and wondered if a skinny little woman could learn how to run a backhoe. Ditch digging had to be easier. With no other jobs and the responsibility of two hungry young children, I stayed in the classroom.

Over time, I learned how to manage behavior in the classroom and how to teach. The first-year horrors were transformed in my mind into amusing anecdotes. Not so with other new teachers. I have watched many caring and intelligent people flee the classroom because they felt overwhelmed or incompetent. Even though I understand why they left, I also think that students in both public and private schools were cheated by these teachers' exodus.

As I gained confidence and skills, my husband, who was a classroom teacher in private and public K–12 schools and who now teaches in the School of Education at a major university, urged me to write a book for teachers, including beginning teachers and teachers who are transferring to another school. I resisted—until I started teaching a U.S. Marine.

For nearly a decade, I have taught behavior management as an adjunct for the University of Virginia. Some of my students are first-year teachers who are newly graduated and realize that their teacher education program left out how to manage student behavior. But most of the students are older, obtaining their teaching license after raising a family or switching to the classroom after a successful and profitable profession in other fields. There are also retired servicemen and servicewomen who decided to serve their country in the classroom. One of my best students, Harry, is a retired Marine, who earned his teaching license a year ago and teaches eighth-grade English. When I saw him recently, I asked him about his job. I wondered specifically how teaching eighth graders compared to his military career. He said, "Patty, I was a Marine, and I served in Vietnam and in the first Gulf War, but for a while last fall, I thought that I'd rather be shot at!"

That's when I decided that I should write this book. Teaching need not be warfare. Even though many administrators refer to their teachers as "the folks in the trenches," we shouldn't feel that every day is a pitched battle. I learned that whether you teach special education, elementary, middle, or high school students, there are many things teachers can do *before* the students step into the classroom, things that make life easier for both teachers and students.

So my intention in writing this book is to address the many problems that I experienced when I began teaching, and to provide guidelines that might prevent the pitfalls that I encountered. However, it is important to understand a simple but abiding fact of life: You will make mistakes. By virtue of your humanity, you will err, and that's okay—*if you learn from your mistakes.* As Geoffrey Colvin of the University of Oregon advises in his video on behavior management, "Don't worry too much if you mess up. You'll have another chance *real soon* to try again."

You will!

ACKNOWLEDGMENTS

The following people have patiently contributed their expertise and encouragement for this book: Ben Sayeski, Kim Dockery, Jay McClain, Charles Ostlund, Kathy Dowd, Carolyn Callahan, Rick Brigham, Stanley Trent, Malcolm Jarrell, and Devery Mock—dedicated educators and good writers all. Thank you!

1

IT'S THE PRINCIPAL OF THE THING

I didn't have an interview with the principal of the school where I taught my first year. Instead, I interviewed with the superintendent, who offered me the option of two jobs. One was as a peripatetic speech pathologist who would see each student for a half hour every other week. The other was as a teacher for students with "mild mental handicaps" in a self-contained class. Without visiting the school or meeting the principal, I signed a contract to teach the class for students with special needs; however, even if I had met with the principal, I would not have known what to ask. If I had known what to ask, my first year might have been less of a nightmare.

In my opinion, principals are the most influential persons in the school systems. They determine the culture of the school, the academic curriculum, the discipline, and the school vision. Even though they must abide by system guidelines, they have wide latitude within those guidelines to develop what some refer to as "the school environment." I taught in the same school for years, and my work environment changed with each new principal. For example, one was adamant that the school building be clean and orderly. She sometimes made surprise "inspections" and demanded that we clean off our desks. (Sometimes I could actually find mine!) Although many of us grumbled about "Sergeant Principal," we noticed that all of us became more organized, that the children kept their classrooms neater, and that parents commented favorably about the "shiny building."

So pay close attention to the principal! Remember that while he or she is interviewing you to determine whether you would be a good match for the school, you're interviewing him or her for the same reason.

BEFORE YOU INTERVIEW: LOOK AROUND

I have visited schools with trailers growing like giant mushrooms around the building. Some trailers have bathrooms; many do not. Some are equipped with phones or intercoms connected to the office; some aren't. Some teachers speak of feeling isolated in the trailers; a few euphemistically refer to the privacy of teaching in a trailer. Whatever the amenities of the trailers, they speak of a building whose population has ballooned beyond that building's capacity. Trailers at a school shouldn't mean that you jump in your car and burn rubber, but their existence should prompt you to ask whether a building program has been approved by the school system, and if so, when a new building might be completed. For example, one school system I visited had to parcel out teachers and students from a middle school to many different schools because of a devastating fire. Although teachers, students, and parents were upset with what one termed "our nonschool," the school board made fast work of obtaining funds from the county board to provide another building, and everyone was aware that this nonschool condition was temporary.

When you do get out of the car, what does the school look like? Recently, I interviewed a principal at a fifty-year-old school in a low socioeconomic area where 80 percent of the students qualify for free lunch. The neighborhood may not be upscale, but the school system has invested in remodeling the school so that it is clean and attractive, inside and out. Teachers and students in the building were smiling, happy, and seemed to enjoy being in school. In other words, the shiny building and the happy teachers and students gave the initial impression that children and teachers mattered to the community.

There's a lot to be gleaned from observing. You should note how the principal and staff are dressed. Is this a coat-and-tie school or a sneakers-and-jeans school? If you feel that a tie is the devil's hangnoose, and all the men are wearing ties, you might be uncomfortable in this school. If you are a jeans-and-T-shirt woman, and everybody is in dresses, hose, and pumps, you might want to interview somewhere else. And while I'm on the subject of dress, please dress appropriately for the interview. That means that the men wear socks with their shoes, pants that fit, and have neatly combed hair. It also means that women wear bras, don't drown themselves in perfume and hairspray, and don't wear anything too tight or too short. And *nobody* wears jeans and sneakers. First impressions are important. An acquaintance who is a principal in a nearby school system related that he had a hard time interviewing a prospective teacher because he was distracted by her appearance. "She had too many jiggly boobs," he complained. I did not ask the obvious question, which is, "How many did she have?"

THE INTERVIEW

When I interviewed principals for this book, I asked what set off alarm bells when they were interviewing applicants. Two said that they had difficulty with what one termed "unrealistic enthusiasm." For example, one assistant principal related, "It is unnerving when applicants say, 'I can teach any grade level.' It makes them sound desperate for a job, but not necessarily *this* job." Another administrator related, "The kiss of death for me is when the applicants say, 'I just love the children with disabilities! They seem to appreciate everything you do for them.' I usually take these candidates on a tour of the building that almost always deposits her or him in the parking lot near the car."

Several topics may be discussed in the initial interview: curriculum, assessment, duties, and discipline. Most interviews last an hour or less, and you cannot possibly find the answers to all the questions posed in this chapter, but you can ask enough to determine whether you are a good match for the school's educational vision. I suggest that you rank the questions that are most important to you and select three or four of the most important ones from each domain. Be prepared to know why you're asking the questions. The administrator who walked the bubbly candidates to the parking lot appreciated applicants' questions, but he usually responded by asking, "That's a good question, why do you ask?" He remembers that the best applicants had excellent reasons for asking each question. The unsuccessful ones had panic attacks and left. They couldn't tell why they wanted answers.

Questions to Ask about Curriculum

The curriculum the school uses has many ramifications for your teaching—so if the principal does *not* mention curriculum, you should.

The principal may want to know what curriculum you have used, either in a previous job or as a student teacher, and many principals want a personal perspective on this curriculum. Specifically, what did you want the children to achieve with this curriculum, and how did you know when you and the students achieved that goal?

What's the school's philosophy about incorporating the state testing into the curriculum? For some schools, the state testing *is* the curriculum. Other schools have a high-achieving population, and the state testing, although important, does not drive all the curricular decisions. What and how you teach may depend on how much emphasis the school places on the state testing. For example, when the curriculum is determined by the state test, all lessons revolve around the test objectives. Some teachers prefer the structure of teaching where the curriculum is set; others prefer more flexibility.

What can you expect if the curriculum in the school is not one with which you are familiar?

- Will there be opportunities for you to learn how to implement the current curriculum from a professional before school starts?
- If you are familiar with the materials the school uses and don't like them, will you be allowed to use another method?
- And if you are allowed to use other curricula, is there funding to purchase other materials?
- Or is the vision of the school locked into using a particular method? If so, how comfortable are you with the philosophy of that method and the strategies used?

For example, a principal at an elementary school whose population is considered at risk for reading failure (many of the students are at least two-years delayed in reading) requires that teachers use Direct Instruction for students in the bottom quartile. Even though the testing results showed that the lower students improved dramatically, some of the teachers detested Direct Instruction and transferred. Those in the school district who enjoyed using this method asked to transfer *to* this school.

Will you be responsible for implementing the curriculum and daily lessons alone, or with a team? When I began my teaching career, there was no emphasis on teams in school systems. We shut the classroom door and tried to survive. Later, school systems gave some of the decision making to the teachers. Textbook adoption and choices of curricula were often made by teams. The prevalence of teams and their influence on school decisions differ from system to system. For example, most high schools and many middle schools have departmental teams that make many curriculum and discipline decisions. Elementary schools may have systemwide team meetings to establish continuity of curricula; however, some school systems have building teams. Other systems do not support teams, and teachers shut their classroom doors and teach what and how they want. So find out whether you will be part of a team or a loner. Some new teachers appreciate the guidance and camaraderie of working with a team and are grateful that curriculum decisions are made as a group. A beginning tenth-grade English teacher said, "I can barely keep my head above water now. If I had to make *all* of these curriculum and lesson plan decisions by myself, I might just drown." Even though the curriculum may be predetermined, the teams may have wide leeway in implementing these curricula. For example, teams often determine which units will be taught, when, and how quickly. A primary school with an affluent population may plan for assessment only for the alphabet objectives on the reading curriculum, and provide only limited instruction to those who need remediation. An inner-city school with an at-risk population may plan to spend more time teaching these skills because the students will not have had the same opportunity to master those objectives.

Often, the team leader will be at the initial job interview and will share the team's expectations of you should you decide to accept the job. Now is the time to ask yourself the following:

- Would I be a good match for the team?
- Do I like the team leader?

- Are the team leader's expectations for a new teacher realistic?
- Does team leadership rotate, and would I have an opportunity for leadership?
- Or are there department chairs rather than team leaders, and how do the chairs earn their positions?

A friend of mine worked in a language department at a high school for seventeen years. For eleven of those years, the team leader was a principal-appointed tyrant who dominated the team and, in my friend's opinion, made some disastrous decisions. She often complained, "He doesn't have the grace to retire and leave us in peace, and he's too mean to die."

Department chairs may earn their positions on the basis of seniority, which means that new teachers are at the bottom of the pecking order. If the department chair is supportive and skilled, that can be a boon to a new teacher. But new teachers can also run into department chairs who resemble the team leader who wouldn't die.

What are the expectations for incorporating technology into the curriculum? How computer literate are the students?

- Is there a computer lab? Do students have regular access to this lab?
- Are there computers in the classrooms?
- What is the percentage of students who have computers at home?
- Are you expected to use computers regularly in your classroom?

An acquaintance of mine recently found a newspaper from the nineteenth century. Its lead article featured the campaign promise of a young man running for the local school board. This aspiring politician not only promised a chalkboard and chalk in every classroom but he also promised to fund workshops so that the teachers could become proficient in this new technology! If you are a techie and the school where you are applying doesn't have much technology, you might want to interview somewhere else.

Questions to Ask about Assessment

Years ago, one of my student teachers expressed horror that I expected her to document her students' skill levels. Not only had the university forgotten to mention assessment to her, but also she couldn't see the need for such an onerous task. She said, "I mean, Patty, suppose some of the kids are not achieving? Then what?!"

"Then we fix it!" I replied.

This wide-eyed princess then became alarmed that we might be "teaching to the test," which in my humble opinion is not a valid complaint. If the concepts are important enough to test, then they are important enough to teach. Should you teach a particular test item? No! Should you teach the concept the item tests? Absolutely!

Formal and informal assessments are vital if we are to determine students' skill levels. Without adequate assessment, students develop gaps and holes in their learning. Some never master the basics as we pile on the deficits. If we don't know what to "fix," we leave the students struggling and getting more and more behind. Or we keep presenting skills that the students have mastered. Neither is good teaching. When students are bored, either because they tune out work that is too hard or because it is too easy for them, they can turn into tyrants who disrupt the classroom.

How does the state department of education in the state in which you are applying administer its tests and how are the results used? Most states require students to take a state-developed test several times during their academic careers.

- How often does this state require testing?
- Is passing the test one of the criteria for student promotion? Or graduation?
- Do students with special needs take the same test as everyone else?
- What are the procedures for determining who takes an alternative test?
- How are the results used?
- How does the state testing influence the curriculum at your school?

Sometimes, the results of these tests may be used to accredit schools, plan remediation for students, obtain additional funding for low-achieving schools, or fire school personnel. In some school systems, assessment results are used as part or all of teacher evaluations. If teacher evaluations are tied to state testing results, it is important for you to determine what support is available for teachers and students in achieving success on these tests.

As previously mentioned, the curriculum for some schools is determined by the state test, and lessons revolve around the test objectives, which may not be complete. For example, social skills training is a major component for students with behavior disorders, but most state tests do not have social skills objectives. One teacher of behavior-disordered students lamented, "I feel so much pressure to stress the academic objectives that there is never enough time to work on the really big issues in my class—social interaction."

What assessments do schools require in addition to state requirements?

- Are there districtwide or systemwide end-of-the-year tests? And if there are other tests, will you have input into what is tested, and how the results are used?
- Does the principal require curriculum-based assessment on a regular basis? Or are you to use a formal assessment instrument? Or both?
- And if you are to use an instrument with which you are unfamiliar, will someone teach you how to use this test *before* the students arrive?

A neighboring school system developed a curriculum-based measurement in reading for elementary students and required that students take the test at least twice per grading period. Administration of the test and record keeping were time consuming and could not have been accomplished without trained volunteers, or without ongoing instruction for new teachers and aides.

What should you do with the information from the tests?

- Do you change academic groupings?
- Does a certain level of assessment trigger a child study referral?
- Is there a school resource that will provide strategies or texts for students who need remediation?
- What are the expectations for teachers when the students don't fit into the curriculum because their achievement is either too high or too low?

What documentation does the school require to validate grades?
Documentation will vary for the different grade levels and from school to school. Tests, reports, quizzes, and homework are possible middle school

and high school yardsticks, while daily seatwork and test results will usually guide elementary grades.

Most administrators want documentation for comments or grades on report cards, particularly if the comments indicate the student is not achieving.

- How many times has the student failed to turn in homework?
- How often have you contacted parents about the problem, and what was their response?
- How many quizzes has the student failed?
- How many times and on what days has a student refused to follow your reasonable requests?

Principals and parents don't like surprises. For example, if one of your students has repeatedly disrupted the class, but the first time the parents hear about their child's misbehavior is a comment on the report card, these parents may be angry. And if the first time the principal knows about the disruptions is when the irritated parents storm into his or her office, clutching the report card, the principal may be irritated also. And the irritation will balloon if you cannot tell the parents and the principal how many times and on which days the misbehavior occurred.

Questions to Ask about Discipline

At a faculty meeting when I was a brand-new teacher, the principal said that he couldn't handle every little burp that happens in the classroom, which prompted a soon-to-be-retired teacher to ask if passing gas would warrant an office referral. Obviously, principals cannot manage the class for you, but you need to know what level of support to expect, and what misbehaviors the principal will handle.

What behaviors will the principal expect you to handle? One principal in a nearby system was quoted as saying, "When you see blood, call me." This principal was not serious, but she was tired of handling what she viewed as minor classroom problems. For example, one teacher at this school would not tolerate a whiff of noncompliance, and if any student refused to complete seatwork, the teacher wrote an office referral. Happy to be sitting in the office looking at the aquarium and getting out of doing their work, students from her class trooped to the office in droves. Other teachers argued with their students and sent members of their class into verbal tantrums, which accelerated into out-of-control classrooms. So ask specifically what behaviors warrant an office referral, and what results you can expect from a referral. For example, will you receive any communication about what punishment, if any, the principal meted out for the incident that caused you to write the referral?

When should I enact a behavior management plan, and are there resources available to help formulate a plan? There are principals who will specifically state when to contact the child study committee (or any other resource in the school) to make a behavior management plan for a student. Others are not so structured; however, every principal should be aware of the resources available to help with children who are delayed academically and socially.

- Who develops behavior plans?
- How frequently are the plans monitored and by whom?

What Other Duties in Addition to My Classroom Preparations and Instruction Am I Expected to Perform?

A new principal observed that I only had eighteen students (the state limit for children with mild mental handicaps was twelve) and also that all my students were integrated for morning homeroom period and lunch—so he decided that I wasn't doing anything. Never mind that I had more than the legal limit of students and no break; this principal said, "You're not doing much" and he assigned me breakfast duty, lunch duty, and a bus line of fifth-grade students, none of whom I knew.

It was always a big shocker for my student teachers to discover that teachers had duties outside of the classroom; one sweet soul even said that when she worked in my classroom, she had mistakenly thought that my extra duties were temporary. Find out what is expected of you. One principal suggested that applicants not verbally attack principals about extra duties but rather euphemistically ask, "What opportunities are there in the school for teacher leadership?" I suggest you *politely* not beat around the bush and find out whether administrators expect you to coach the girls' volleyball team. Or will you be the playground teacher every other day? In one school, the principal required all support staff to do the extras: breakfast duty, lunch duty, bus duty, and monitoring the halls. So the librarian, the physical education teacher, the music teacher, the special education staff, and the speech therapist (who was in the school two half days a week) had all the grunt jobs. This was a great arrangement for the classroom teachers, but not so nice for the support staff who taught seven classes a day with no break. And don't be confused by state regulations that mandate that teachers have duty-free lunches. Legislatures are famous for mandating but not funding.

The truth of the matter is that in order for a school to function safely and smoothly, *everybody* has to do more than teach their classes. Just find out *before* you take a job what extras you will have.

But do find out if there are opportunities for leadership. Could you help form a parent/teacher liaison for better cooperation with parents? Will the school adopt new texts soon, and if so, could you be on the adoption committee? Don't ignore leadership opportunities, but also, don't be deluded. *Lunch duty is not a leadership opportunity.*

What Opportunities Does the School System Offer?

What are the financial resources of the system?   Throughout your career, in addition to the periodic course work required by states in order to renew your license, you may want to improve your skills by taking graduate-level courses or attending workshops and conferences. These all cost money.

- Will the school system reimburse you for successfully completing recertification hours?
- If you enroll in a graduate program, are there funds available for reimbursement?
- What types of staff development does the school system support, and will any of these staff development workshops apply toward recertification?
- Will you be supported for attending professional conferences?

What Other Stuff Should I Ask About?

Much of the information about the school may be in the school handbook, but if it isn't, ask.

What is the average length of service for teachers in the school?

• Why are teachers transferring or leaving the school?

There are lots of reasons why teachers transfer or retire early. Some teachers become so attached to the principal that if he or she leaves, the teachers don't want to stay in that school anymore. Some areas have a high turnover rate because the community is a transient society. For example, a school system in a college town might employ many of the spouses of the graduate students at the college—but when the students graduate, the family moves.

There are schools where the turnover rate is high because the administration is too demanding or unsupportive. There are also schools where the discipline is nonexistent, which makes teachers and students feel edgy and unsafe. In one situation in my local district, teachers transferred from a school because they didn't want to use the curriculum the principal demanded that they use.

How many students are enrolled in the school, and what is the approximate average class size? A special education teacher I know had twenty-one students in her class for students with special needs. The legal limit for the particular disability of students she taught was a class size of twelve, but the superintendent kept writing waivers, and the state kept approving the waivers. She wearily expressed that she had too many individuals to individualize. Some school systems take pride in keeping class size manageable. Others have no choice but to shove more desks into a room. Smaller class size means more classrooms and more teachers, and some schools simply do no have the space for one more classroom. For example, the population at a school in an affluent neighborhood suddenly outgrew the building. This burgeoning population surprised the administrators, and they were caught with a mess. At first, the special education classes were moved to "quiet corners" in the hall so that there were more classrooms for regular education. Then, as the children kept coming, they gave the quiet corners to regular education classes and moved the special education classes to closets! I am thankful that this situation doesn't happen with regularity, and that this system resolved the problem, but it was a nightmare for students and teachers!

What are the risk factors at the school?

- What is the overall socioeconomic status of the students?
- How many students qualify for free lunch?
- What is the percentage of parents with high school diplomas?

Schools whose populations are from middle socioeconomic or affluent neighborhoods present different problems than schools whose population is less affluent. Poverty is hard on children. It may mean poor housing, poor or nonexistent medical care, lack of supervision, no telephones, and often inadequate clothing. Poverty may also mean that parents must live in high crime areas where children are exposed to daily violence.

Parents who have not completed high school might have difficulty understanding school newsletters and notes, might not respond to written communication, and therefore might appear disinterested in their children's progress. For example, Andy, one of my students, never came to school the first day after a vacation. Andy finally confided, "My momma don't know when she's 'sposed to wash my clothes and get me ready for the bus." His mother could not read well, worked three part-time jobs, and was always unaware of when her children were to return to school. Thereafter, whenever there was an extended holiday, I sent home a calendar with a crayon attached, and Andy crossed off each day when he got up in the morning. I colored in the day he was to return so that he knew when to wash clothes and get ready for school. He said, "It's like a library book, ain't it, Ms. Pullen? I just have to know the due date."

There are different problems with upper socioeconomic parents. Often, the children from these homes are busy, busy, busy. I have watched in awe as parents fetched their children for some activity every afternoon after school. There is a frenzy of carting children to soccer practice, music lessons, ballet lessons, art instruction, foreign language instruction, and on and on and on. I felt sorry for one third-grade girl who pleaded with her mother, "Do I have to go to Spanish lessons? Can't I just play this afternoon?" This prompted a teaching assistant to quip, "Some of our students are underneglected."

Are there many children from single parent families? I was a single parent, so I harbor no prejudices about single parents; however, I also remember how hard it was to supervise my children and earn a living. Sometimes, single parents cannot supervise their children adequately, and if there is no extended family to take up the slack, many children are left to monitor themselves. Unsupervised children might not complete homework or study for tests, and more important, they might find illegal or unsafe ways to amuse themselves. I still remember meeting an eight-year-old on our downtown mall one Friday evening around midnight. He was alone, very dirty, panhandling, and smoking a cigarette. Initially, I was more stunned that he was inhaling than that he was a second grader without supervision on the mall late at night. This child's mother worked a late shift and depended on her older son to supervise her eight-year-old. He didn't.

An associated problem with single parents is that it is often difficult to arrange a conference with them. Many do not have phones, notes often don't make the trip home, and some single parents work more than one job so you can't find them. This does *not* mean that single parents do not care for their children—but it does mean that they are often overwhelmed.

What are the school procedures for dealing with risk and other problems?

- What should you do if you suspect one of your students is abused?
- What should you do if a student threatens suicide? Some school systems have strict guidelines for reporting suspected abuse or threats of suicide.
- What should you do if you suspect a student has a weapon?
- What should you do if a student becomes ill or hurt?
- What should you do if you're ill?
- What is your role in the safety and security of the school? Are there lockdowns? Are there evacuation plans?

- When should you write a special education referral?
- What is the division policy regarding retention?

How many support staff work in the school?

- Does the school have a nurse? If so, does he come every day or does he serve several schools?
- Is there a guidance counselor at the school?
- Is there a school psychologist? If so, is she available to help with behavior management plans or does testing consume all of her time?

You will probably not have time during the initial interview to determine all the answers to the questions posed here, but sometime between the interview and signing a contract, you should read the school handbook and find many of the answers, providing that the principal will give you a copy of the handbook. Ask for one, but don't be chagrined if the principal won't give you a handbook before you are hired. For one thing, some handbooks are large and too expensive to give to every aspiring applicant. For another, some principals prefer to read *every word* of the handbook in the fall at the first faculty meeting during teacher workweek. (This is *not* a fabrication.) In fairness to these principals who drone on for hours, they read the handbook to us because we never read it. Read the handbook.

SUMMARY

In my opinion, principals are the most important people in the school system, and principals interview prospective job applicants. It is important to interview the principals while they are interviewing you. Find out the following information:

- What curriculum does the school use? Is there help if you're unfamiliar with this curriculum?
- What assessments are used and will the principal expect you to administer tests?

- What behavior problems will the principal expect to handle?
- What other duties besides classroom instruction will you be expected to manage?
- What opportunities for leadership does the school system offer?
- What miscellaneous questions (e.g., number of single mothers in the student body) are important to you?
- Do the faculty and staff seem happy?

2

GET THE SCOOP!

A popular educational philosophy is to "discover" your students rather than seek information about them. Teachers I know have "discovered" the most amazing things about their students! When one student wrecked a fifth-grade classroom, the teacher "discovered" that the student qualified as a student with severe emotional disturbance. The case manager for this student forgot to tell the teacher that this integrated student was a student with special needs—and that he was "a bit violent sometimes."

Some teachers think that gathering information about students is prejudging them, or developing preconceived and possibly damaging opinions. However, if you search for information in a professional and ethical manner, and use that information to preplan for academic and social success, you have given your students a leg up in your class and saved yourself some end-of-the-day headaches. We expect physicians, dentists, lawyers, counselors, and other professionals to know our histories so that they can help us without making stupid mistakes. It makes good sense for teachers to know what other people have experienced or found out about our students.

Sources of information about your students are school faculty and staff, the cumulative folder, psychological folders, and the parents. Use them all.

You can't know too much—but you need to realize that sometimes information may be wrong. However, if you don't have the information, you can't even make that judgment.

But what are you looking for and how will you know when you find it? You are looking for your "tough kids"—the students who will have the most difficulty academically and socially. These are the students that you need to preplan for—the ones who need the most help.

Probably the defining characteristic of a tough kid is noncompliance. "Noncompliance is simply defined as not following a direction within a reasonable amount of time" (Rhode, Jenson, and Reavis 1993, 4). Some describe noncompliance as the "kingpin" around which all other behavioral excesses revolve (Rhode et al. 1993, 3). I agree. Many tough kids engage us; they suck us into arguments by refusing to comply with simple and reasonable requests. They get a big payoff for their noncompliance: they get out of work, they control the classrooms. Yet they pay the price for noncompliance with academic and social deficits. You can spot the academic delays in the school records, and sometimes the social deficits show up in the form of office referrals. You can also glean a lot of information with "teacher talk."

Where Do I Get Information?

What is "teacher talk"? How do you talk to other professionals about your students in an ethical and professional manner? An angry art teacher stormed into my classroom one morning with one of my mainstreamed students, "Harry," who had completely disrupted her second-grade class. She demanded that he never return to art class without supervision. When I asked her to describe his misbehavior, she said, "He got bored with the project, stood on the table, pulled down his pants, and showed everybody Mr. Happy!" Apparently, two little girls in the class were so alarmed by "Mr. Happy" that they cried, while the boys hooted.

Even though the art teacher was very angry, she was succinct in her description and offered no judgment about the child, or so I thought. When I came into the teachers' lounge later that day, the collected faculty was hee-hawing about Harry's episode in art class, and I realized that Harry's Mr. Happy was a subject of schoolwide hilarity. I have to admit that I had laughed about what my aide termed, "Harry's exposé." Sometimes it's important to laugh about what kids do (otherwise you're humorless and depressed). However, it's never okay to ridicule a child or encourage the ridicule by others. The criteria for telling others about classroom incidents should be (a) helping to plan and implement a strategy for managing behavior or (b) seeking support. Unfortunately, the art teacher's relating the incident to other teachers didn't help to plan and implement a strategy to prevent Harry's future misbehavior, nor was the art teacher seeking support for an unpleasant incident.

So how do you share information about a student? How do you talk to other professionals so that you meet the preceding criteria?

- Do other professionals understand that you will maintain confidentiality of the information they give you?
- Do other professionals understand that you will use and share information to plan for academic or social improvement?
- Do other professionals understand that you will not ridicule or demean the student to anyone on the basis of the information they give?
- Do the parents have access to or knowledge of the information given to you?

When teachers suspect parents of abuse, they often filter the information they give parents; you should be aware of what has been shared with the parents, how that information was shared, and why.

Why is your class roll important, and who will help you with it? When I pulled my class roll from my box at my first job, another teacher looked over my shoulder and said, "Oh, my!" I didn't take the hint and run to someone who could give me information about my class—information that could have helped me preplan for a successful year. Pay close attention to your class roll. It's not just a list of names, it's your life for the next ten months!

Some school systems have team leaders who attend the induction workshops for new teachers, and these leaders share pertinent information about class rolls to the inductees. Other systems have departmental meetings during the workweek when teachers share information about students. For example, fourth-grade teachers might meet with fifth-grade teachers to share information about the rising fifth graders. This is usually when teachers will suggest that Johnny and Harry not sit next to each other, or that Susie's mother is a very concerned parent who will observe in the classroom three mornings a week.

But someone should be available to tell you important facts about your students—facts that may not appear in the cumulative folders or other reports, facts that will make your life easier in the classroom. For example, two second-grade girls transferred into my class from a class for students with developmental delays. When the sending teacher briefed me on my new students, she told me that the competition between these girls was unbelievably disruptive. She advised that I keep them as far away from each other as possible. I planned accordingly: seated the girls across the room from each other, mainstreamed them in separate classrooms, and placed them in different academic groups. They had few opportunities to interact and therefore disrupt. If there is no mention that someone will brief you about your class roll, ask who can.

- Will the principal or assistant principal have an opportunity to help?
  1) In schools with small populations, the principal and the assistant principal may brief you about your students.
- Who else has knowledge of your students?
  1) Is there a curriculum instructor in the school?
  2) Is there a guidance counselor? Guidance counselors are familiar with the troubled students—students who failed academically or socially, or both.
  3) Is there a previous teacher mentioned in the cumulative folder who can give me information about my students?
  4) Is there a school nurse who might have information?
  5) Is there an instructional assistant who would have information?

When you are new to a school and you barely know where the coffeepot and the bathrooms are, have no idea of the names of half of the faculty, are overwhelmed with preschool workshops and paperwork, then contacting members of the faculty for information about your students can be daunting. Some teachers use a form letter that they put in mailboxes of the teachers whose conversations and records indicate may have information about their tough kids. The following is an example:

Date: Aug. 25

To: Mr. Helpful

From: Patty Pullen (10th grade science)

About: Johnny Buck

Johnny Buck is on my class roll for this year, and Mr. Principal tells me that you may have some insights into how to help Johnny succeed this year. May we meet at your convenience about Johnny? I have workshops tomorrow and Thursday mornings, but I am free every afternoon this week.

Times you can meet:

_____

Where you would like to meet:

_____

Some teachers will ignore these requests. Others may write that they don't have the time to meet with you. Some may give you their home phone number and ask that you contact them at home. Others may return your letter with a cryptic note stating that they have no insights. One teacher who could not find the time to meet with me wrote, "May the force be with you!" My aide found that comment "very insightful!" However, most professionals want the best for their students, past and present, and will *make* time to meet with you.

And don't forget e-mail. Most school systems have e-mail, which can be a time-saver when trying to contact teachers at another school in the system.

What Do You Want to Learn? What Do You Ask?

If you are a high school teacher who will be teaching more than a hundred students, you can't learn about *all* of your students, but you can determine pertinent information about *some* of them. And if you're an elementary or special education teacher, you may learn some important facts about all of your students.

- Are any of your students noncompliant? Noncompliance (not complying with adults' requests or instructions) is the "kingpin" behavior that facilitates tough kids' disruptive and excessive behaviors.
  1) If so, is there a particular activity or naturally occurring reinforcer that the student will work for?
  2) What forms of mild nonphysical punishment, such as withholding privileges, have been effective?
- How supportive of the school and teachers are the parents?
- What are the social strengths or weaknesses of the student?
  1) Is the student a leader?
  2) Is the student a bully?
  3) Is the student a loner? Or, does he or she have lots of friends?
  4) Does the student dominate class discussions, or does he wait to be called on? Or does the student appear threatened when asked to respond in class?
  5) Is the student disruptive during academic instruction? If so, is she better behaved in one subject than in others?
  6) Is the student better behaved for one teacher than others?
  7) Does the student explode during unstructured activities, such as recess or lunch?
  8) Who are the buddies or friends of the tough kid, and are these buddies and friends difficult also?
- Are there family issues that may contribute to misbehavior that may not be in the school records?
  1) Has there been a recent death in the family?
  2) Has there been a recent divorce?
  3) Is there a new baby in the house?
  4) Is there a new stepparent in the family?

5) Has the student ever been removed from the home because of neglect or abuse?
- What academic interventions have been used with the student?
  1) Has the student been in Title I?
  2) Has the student had instruction in English as a Second Language?
  3) Is the student enrolled in any other pullout program?
  4) Is the student achieving in some academic areas but not in others?
- Are any of the students on the class roll nonreaders?

When I worked as a substitute teacher, I often taught in a private middle school. The first time I taught there, the teacher's lesson plans stated that students were to take turns reading orally and discussing the social studies text; however, the teacher failed to inform me that one of her students was a nonreader and would become disruptive if urged to participate. I found that out when I inadvertently humiliated the nonreader and myself, and precipitated a giant disruption in the classroom. Nonreaders are often the most noncompliant and the toughest students; unfortunately, nonreaders are prevalent in our school systems.

What Are Cumulative Folders and Why Are They Important?

The first cumulative folders that I waded through were very creative, if lacking in substance. I found this note in one student's folder: "Johnny is impotent in the classroom." After reading this note, I zipped into the principal's office with the hope that Johnny, a fifteen-year-old, was potent outside of the classroom, or that something could be done to alter this sad situation. I also puzzled how the teacher who wrote the note had determined the sexual dysfunction of the student in the classroom, or why a teacher would want a student to function sexually in the classroom! I realized that my naiveté had no bounds when the principal, with only a hint of a smile, said that the teacher probably meant that Johnny was "impudent."

Since parents have acquired the privilege of reading their child's folder, these cumulative records have changed drastically, and it is rare that teachers find the unsupported and prejudicial comments that I routinely stumbled upon in my early teaching.

However, some of these folders can be several inches thick, particularly if the student is in high school—so what do you look for and why are you looking for it? And if you're a high school teacher, can you possibly read all the folders of students on your class roll? Probably not! But you can read the folders of the students who faculty and staff have indicated may present problems in the classroom.

What basic information does the cumulative folder contain that may be important to you in the classroom?

- Is there pertinent medical information in the folder?
  1) Is the student diabetic?
  2) Does the student have seizures?
  3) Does the student take prescription drugs for ADHD, such as Ritalin?
  4) Does the student take any other medication for a serious illness?
  5) Does the student have a visual or auditory impairment?
  6) Is the student morbidly obese?

If the answer to any of the preceding questions is yes, you should talk with the school nurse about the medical condition and how to handle this in the classroom. For example, one fifth-grade teacher and a diabetic student developed a signal when the student was to go to the resource room to eat his snack, which he was embarrassed to do in front of the class. You should also discuss some of these medical conditions with the parents. What you need to know is how this medical condition will affect the student's functioning in the classroom and how you will need to adapt the classroom environment for the student.

- Is the student in foster care or has he ever been in foster care?
  1) Is the student in foster care because of neglect or abuse, or because of illness or the death of a parent?
- Does the student qualify for special education services? Is there a separate psychological folder for this student?
- Has the student ever been evaluated for services as a child with disabilities but did not qualify for services?
- Does the student attend school regularly? If the attendance is sporadic, why?

1) Are absences due to illness?
2) Are absences due to family pressures, such as baby-sitting or pro-
tecting an abused parent?
3) Are absences due to neglectful parents who are not committed to
their child going to school regularly?

Buried in the back of the folder of one of my new students was a letter from protective services instructing the school to contact them whenever the student was absent. Regular attendance is important, and if the student does not attend regularly and does not have a medical condition, then why is he or she consistently absent? The answers to the preceding will probably not be in the cumulative folder, but they should prompt you to chase down the school social worker for the facts.

• Has the student attended many different schools?
1) If so, why? Are the parents in military service?
2) Does the parent have a job that requires the family to move often?
3) Are parents on the move to keep a step ahead of protective services?

Whatever the reason for many transfers, changing schools often is hard for children and sometimes predicts low academic achievement and/or be-havior problems. If the student's parents are not moving because of job re-quirements, they may be trying to outrun protective services, who suspect abuse, or they may be escaping an abusive spouse who is stalking them. Be particularly watchful of those students.

• Does the student have siblings?
1) How many siblings are there?
2) Do any of the student's siblings attend the same school?
3) If the student is a "tough kid," are any of his siblings also considered "tough kids"?
• What names of professionals who have worked with the student are in
the folder, and why are these names important?

You look for names of professionals because they may have pertinent in-formation about the student—information that they will not place in the folder. For example, I became very frustrated trying to meet with the mother of one of my new students. Even though this mother routinely made appointments for both home visits and school conferences, she always stood me up. When I spoke with the visiting teacher from the child's previous school, he told me that the mother prostituted herself for drugs, and that the grandmother was the responsible adult to contact because the children lived with her, even though she was not considered the legal guardian.

- Is there a separate discipline folder?
  1) If so, where is the discipline folder kept?

Sometimes discipline folders are locked in the principal's office and teachers are not aware that there is a discipline folder. If there is a discipline folder, it records the serious misbehavior(s) that might have precipitated a suspension or expulsion. You need to know just how tough your tough kids are.

What do I do with the information from the folder?   Another popular educational philosophy is that teachers should not compare students; however, comparing students is the basic philosophy for much of the state testing required by the No Child Left Behind dictum. Comparisons are a normal and even necessary part of teaching. When you read the cumulative folders, however, you are going to use the information in the folders to compare the student with himself or herself. You are looking for patterns of behavior that will affect school achievement.

- What academic comparisons can you make?
  1) Has the student *usually* achieved academically?
  2) Has the student *rarely* achieved academically?
  3) Is the student failing now, but there was a time when he or she was successful? If so, why is the student failing now?
  4) Is the student significantly better in one subject than another?
  5) If the student qualifies as a special needs student, has his or her academic performance improved since placement in a program for students with disabilities? Or has the student's achievement declined?
  6) If the student is in foster care, after a period of adjustment, has his or her academic achievement improved since removal from home?

- What behavioral and social comparisons can you make?
  1) Does the student consistently misbehave at specific times or for specific teachers?
  2) Has the student routinely been a behavior problem or was there a time when she was compliant?
  3) If the student qualifies as a student with disabilities, has his behavior improved since placement?
  4) If the student is in foster care, has her behavior improved since removal from the home?

Comparing the information in the folder may indicate that the academic or social programs implemented for the student need revision, or this information may show that a student needs a full evaluation for possible placement as a student with special needs, or the data may indicate that the Department of Social Services should step in and provide protection.

For example, carefully read the report cards that are usually in the cumulative folder. Low grades accompanied by big changes in behavior for students who have previously achieved at a high level may mean that the student has experienced a family trauma—death, divorce, moving, new baby, or remarriage of a parent—and that the low achievement or behavior is temporary. Or it could be an indication that he or she developed a major illness—which you could document by checking the medical information in the folder. It could also mean that the student's friends are not into academics and peer pressure is responsible for the decline. Low grades could also mean that the material has gotten too hard and the student may need help, particularly if the low grades continue over a year and are accompanied by an increase in misbehavior. Whatever the reason for the decline in grades, previous grades indicate that at one time the student was capable of achieving and might succeed again if the proper adaptations were made.

If the student has always earned below-average grades, he or she may have low cognitive functioning and need help or the student may be from a chaotic family that doesn't value education, so neither does he or she. Both possibilities require some preplanning in order to motivate the student, and may even require that you refer the student to the child study committee.

If the student is significantly better in one subject than another, he or she may have a mild learning disability and may misbehave during instruction in order to escape feeling inadequate. When I asked one of my lunch-duty students why I always had to retrieve him from the office for lunch, he told me that that's when he had language arts. When I asked what language arts had to do with his being sent to the office every day before lunch, he asked, "Who wants to sit around and feel dumb?" Author Frank McCourt, who was an English teacher in a high school in the Bronx, says that he finally understood that his students' off-task questions were specifically intended to avoid studying English.

If a student is in foster care, read the folder with great care. You want to determine if the student's behavior and academic achievement has improved during foster care, or is the student angry, noncompliant, and disinterested in academics. It is an unfortunate fact that many foster homes are as abusive as the ones from which the students have been removed. Also, the attachment children have for their parents is so strong that even if the parents have been abusive, many children want to return home and are often very angry because they can't. Whatever the case, even if the student seems happy and adjusted with the foster care parents, contact the social worker. The social worker is your link with the foster parents, the natural parents, and the safety net for your student, should he or she show up bruised. *Be extra vigilant with your foster care students.*

When I retired from the classroom, I became a Court Appointed Special Advocate (CASA) volunteer for children who are removed from the home for abuse and neglect. My first case was a tenth-grade girl, "Anna," who was removed from the home because of parental abuse. I met with the guidance counselor at Anna's school so that I could read the cumulative folder. I wanted to learn the names of Anna's teachers for future reference about Anna's behavior and academic progress. When the counselor handed me Anna's folder, she told me that she had just reviewed it and was puzzled by "some special education information" in the folder.

The special education information was very instructive. When Anna was in the first grade, her mother abandoned her, her father was in drug rehab, and she lived with an aunt for over a year. In the second grade, she qualified as a student with severe emotional disturbance, and her aunt signed placement papers for Anna to receive academic help and counseling. After a court battle, Anna's father obtained custody at the end of Anna's third year in school. Then the father moved and enrolled Anna in fourth grade as a regular education student. She almost failed the fourth grade, but steadily improved academically thereafter. Even though there were special education documents in her folder from the second grade, there was no mention of her ever receiving services in the new system, or of her being staffed out of special education. When I called the special education office in this system, they had no information about Anna.

When I interviewed Anna, I remarked that she had been in special education but had steadily improved without services. I wondered if she thought that she had been identified erroneously because she improved dramatically after moving with her father. She said, "Mrs. Pullen, I didn't dare get bad grades. Daddy made that painful."

Anna abandoned society and lived on the streets for a while. I could never stop worrying that maybe if she had had a case manager, someone who would have demanded that she get counseling for her issues of abandonment, or a teacher she trusted to whom she could have confided her father's abuse—then maybe she would not have spent time on the street and later in drug rehab.

Read the folders.

SUMMARY

In order to preplan for tough kids, teachers should have every scrap of information they can find about these students. Teachers can find this information from the following sources:

- Other professionals who have knowledge of the student
- Student records, including cumulative folders
- Parents

The information should be used to compare the student with his or her past academic and social achievement in order to better plan for the student's success.

CHAPTER 2

REFERENCE

Rhode, G., W. R. Jenson, and K. R. Reavis. 1993. *The tough kid book: Practical classroom management strategies.* Longmont, Colo.: Sopris West.

3

PARENTS!
WHO NEEDS THEM?

You do! "The involvement of parents in the education of their children is of unquestionable significance. Scores of studies indicate that student achievement increases as parents become more involved in their children's education" (Whitaker and Fiore 2001, 15).

Educational research is replete with references to the positive effects of parent collaboration for both academic and social achievement. According to Dr. Hill Walker and his colleagues of the University of Oregon, the number one way to raise students' achievement at school is to involve parents. "Although it is possible to effect positive behavioral changes in school without involving parents in the intervention, any behavior gains achieved in a school-only intervention will likely be specific to that setting" (Walker, Colvin, and Ramsey 1995, 268).

Although most teachers and administrators know the value of parent collaboration in our schools, most states do not require a course in parent involvement for licensure—so teachers are left with their instincts for a road map when dealing with parents. And for some, the road map seems to lead to pain, if not to perdition. Teachers are instructed to involve parents and to engender trust, but without many guidelines for accomplishing these goals. This is particularly difficult when we must try to collaborate with parents who are from different ethnic backgrounds, different races, different socio-economic backgrounds, or hold different values than we do. We either don't know how or don't consider it important to admit to and examine our prejudices about these many differences. Without this self-realization, we may inadvertently make a mess of our attempts to collaborate with parents. I have heard teachers lament that they would rather have a root canal than interact with their students' parents!

How different from when I grew up! There was a close relationship between my teachers, my parents, and the parents of my classmates.

When I was in the fourth grade, my best friend and I planned a scientific experiment. We wondered if bulls chased only red or if they were stimulated by movement, so we each took a scarf, one red and the other blue, and headed into the field with the Dennys' bull. Our parents had threatened us with spankings if we were foolish enough to set foot in the field with the bull and lived to tell the tale, but science won over threats of a spanking. The bull didn't wait for us to wave our scarves, but thundered after us as soon as he saw us. We barely escaped by diving over a barbed-wire fence, which tore our clothes and our skin. Afraid to mention our adventure (we had never been spanked and didn't want to be), we doctored ourselves, ate with our gloves on so no one would know that we had hurt our hands and ask how, and had recurring nightmares about this monstrous bull. When I developed a fever and red streaks on my arms, my teacher made me take off my gloves and sent me to Miss Nettie, the principal. I tearfully told Miss Nettie how I'd hurt myself, and she called my father to take me to the doctor. I still remember her side of the conversation.

"Lynwood, Patty has been in the field with the Dennys' bull. She is injured and needs to see a doctor. Lynwood, don't you touch this child! And furthermore, don't you fuss at her. She has suffered enough and knows never to be so stupid again."

My father took me to the doctor and never mentioned the episode! When the doctor began to lecture me on the foolishness of my scientific experiment, my father said, "Miss Nettie says not to fuss at her, Doc."

The doctor said, "Oh, okay!"

When I started teaching, I often wished that I had the respect, trust, and power that Miss Nettie had with the parents of her students. But in retrospect, it is important to remember that it was a very different time. All but one of my teachers had either grown up with my parents or had taught them. I saw my teachers in the grocery stores, at church, at the movies, and in my parents' living room. They were neighbors and friends, and their children were my playmates. This is not the case now. There are many differences between families today and in past generations.

WHO ARE THE PARENTS OF YOUR STUDENTS?

Before you can get a handle on your tough kids, you need to know about family configurations in general—and your tough kids' families specifically.

What Are the Family Configurations of the Twenty-First Century?

Do many of the mothers of your students work?

- According to the Bureau of Labor Statistics, in 1940, less than 9 percent of all women with children worked outside the home.
- According to the Bureau of Labor Statistics, in 1997, 76.5 percent of women with children between the ages of six and thirteen were employed outside the home (http://stats.bls.gov).

Are any of the mothers of your students single?

- In 2001, one in three American babies was born to a single mother due to the increase in the divorce rate and women giving birth out of wedlock (Annie E. Casey Foundation 2003).

There are numerous reasons why mothers are in the labor force, one of which is economic necessity. It's becoming increasingly more difficult to raise a family on one income. Also, the rise in divorce demands that women work to provide for their children, and sometimes their income is barely above the poverty level. Most single mothers are the only caretaker, which places both economic and emotional stress on the family. In the last several years, fatherless children tripled to 17 million, and this absence of fathers produces profound problems for our schools (Connecticut Department of Social Services). "In fact, children from fatherless homes have been found to be both less productive in school and responsible for a high percentage of criminal behavior" (Whitaker and Fiore 2001, 18).

According to the Department of Social Services of Connecticut, children from fatherless homes are at greater risk for lifelong adjustment problems.

Did you know that children who live without contact with their biological fathers, when compared to other kids, are:

- five times more likely to live in poverty;
- more likely to bring drugs and weapons to school;
- twice as likely to commit a crime;
- twice as likely to drop out of school;
- twice as likely to be abused;
- more likely to run away from home (boys 63 percent more);
- more likely to commit suicide;
- twice as likely to abuse drugs and alcohol;
- twice as likely to end up in jail;
- four times more likely to need help for emotional or behavioral problems; and
- more likely to become pregnant as a teenager and start the welfare cycle all over again. (Connecticut Department of Social Services, www.dss.state.ct.us)

What are the economic stresses on single family configurations?

- Child care
- Unpaid child support
- Homelessness

According to the U.S. Bureau of the Census, poor families with an employed mother who paid for child care spent roughly three times as much of their budget on child care as families who were not poor—20 percent versus 7 percent—and 36 percent of poor families had no regular arrangement for care (www.census.gov). In Virginia, 225,000 parents owe their children more than $1.93 billion in child support (www.dss.state.va.us), which may account for the fact that the U.S. Bureau of the Census reported that in 1999, 41 percent of single mothers who are heads of the household live in poverty.

Added to this depressing economic picture, the National Center for Homeless Education reports that some of our children are homeless. In 1998, there were over 615,000 homeless children in the United States, and 45 percent of these homeless children (K–12) do not attend school regularly (www.serve.org/nche/SEASdata.htm).

If you're teaching in a rural area, don't be deluded that homelessness is an urban problem. "Though we traditionally think of this as primarily an urban dilemma, these proportions are likely to be even higher in rural areas" (Whitaker and Fiore 2001, 18).

The economic stresses on families may mean that parents are overwhelmed with concern about how to pay the rent, feed their children, and buy clothing. They may not have the time or the energy to volunteer in the schools or to do anything more than monitor homework. They may be working several jobs and not have time or the transportation to come to school for a conference. But they still love their children.

I was a single mother when my son was in the second grade. One Friday afternoon, he handed me a note from the principal, who demanded that I call her immediately because James had brought medicine to school. I called the principal at work and at her home repeatedly that weekend, but never got her. This was before the days of message machines, so there was no evidence that I had tried repeatedly to contact her. James admitted that he had had a terrible headache Friday morning, didn't want to burden me, and so took a small bottle of aspirin to school.

On Sunday evening, the principal called. She was furious with me because I had not called her and made sarcastic comments about "women who try to go it alone." This principal never asked me whether I knew that James had brought aspirin to school. Nor would she listen to my explanation or apology. She just told me off—or harangued me.

Even though I knew this was not the best choice for my children's academic success, I never set foot in that school again. I could trust the school to do two things: 1) judge me unfairly, and 2) not listen to me. Don't make the same mistakes.

This incident flames in my mind today, and I wonder how parents can negotiate with teachers and with school systems effectively if they feel as powerless as I did. And is this feeling of powerlessness more prominent for poor families, particularly the single mothers?

You cannot do anything about your students' family life, nor can you alter their economic plight. However, you can alter your expectations of these parents and not expect them to volunteer in your class, accompany the class on field trips, or bake cookies for the class party. You can treat them with respect, and you can keep them informed about their children. But most importantly, listen to your parents. Even though we often view these parents as not attentive at best, or neglectful at worst, most parents care deeply for their children. Some are overwhelmed, and often their apparent lack of attention to their children covers a more troubling problem.

Are any of your students from a cultural or ethnic background that is different from yours?

- Are the majority of your students from Anglo-European descent?
- Are any of your students Asian?
- Are any of your students Native American?
- Are any of your students African American?
- Are any of your students Hispanic?
- Are any of your students of mixed ethnicity?

Most of us want to be culturally competent and to understand multicultural issues, but it is my opinion that most of us aren't and don't. I was dumbstruck a few years ago when an African American friend of mine blamed the high, single-mother birthrate among African American teenagers on integration. She said that when she was growing up in the 1960s, it was most unusual for a single girl to get pregnant, and that this trend was due to the "interactions with whites and their loose morals." She was surprised when I told her that the white folks in my small hometown never condoned sex-when-not-married and considered having children without benefit of clergy a disgrace!

I can't throw stones at my African American friend because until I was in my twenties, I thought that black folks couldn't get sunburned, and I was always confused when I saw an African American buying suntan lotion! Now I'm embarrassed at my stupidity. Most of us tend to stereotype different cultures, ethnicities, and races based on what we have learned from our families and from the media, and we often accept these sometimes distorted observations as the gospel. It can be a mind-numbing experience to have to rethink an issue.

I can't provide a course in multicultural education here, nor do I wish to stereotype any ethnic group, but there are a few tips that might help when you interact with parents. For example, Asians are the fastest growing minority in the United States. Many Asian countries are represented in our schools, and most Asian cultures highlight the importance of the family. "The concern for maintaining the interdependence of the family and the individual's loyalty to the family is seen in child-rearing practices. Behaviors of the individual are seen as reflecting on one's ancestors and one's race" (Springate and Stegelin 1999, 107).

"Some think that a quiet, structured environment is appropriate for our Asian population, and that the informality between teachers and students may be confusing" (Springate and Stegelin 1999, 108).

Because there are many Native American tribes, each with differing customs, it is important that teachers carefully research the cultural practices of the families of their Native American students to learn how these families view education, how they might be expected to collaborate with teachers, and their style of communication. Among many American Indian tribes, the extended family often shares the responsibility of raising children, and older family members are consulted about child-rearing practices.

Also, remember that in some tribes, there is mistrust of school personnel because of the boarding schools in the nineteenth and twentieth centuries when children were removed from their homes, transported long distances, and abused if they spoke their native language or practiced their customs. Although the purpose of the schools was to give the children a marketable skill that they could use in the mainstream of society and therefore "assimilate," the schools robbed these children of their language, religion, and culture by severely punishing them if they practiced the customs of their tribes. Some blame the boarding schools for the increase in alcoholism among our Native Americans, robbed of one culture but not fitting into another.

Hispanics presently are the largest minority in the United States. Although there are immigrants from South America and the Caribbean, most Hispanics in the United States are from Mexico, Puerto Rico, and Cuba. As with the other cultures in our society, even though there are numerous Hispanic cultures represented in the United States, we can make some generalities. Many share the same religion: Catholicism. There is also an emphasis on the family and how an individual's behavior will reflect on the family. "Although education is valued, its goal is for the benefit of the family and not simply for the individual. Should education come between the individual and the family, it may receive a low priority" (Springate and Stegelin 1999, 108).

The history of enslavement and oppression has had long-term effects for many African Americans, and some have had difficulty moving beyond this legacy. Again, we should avoid stereotypic descriptions, but according to some writers, "Endurance of suffering while moving ahead is a major theme found in Black families" (Springate and Stegelin 1999). One writer relates how African Americans have been able to survive under such harsh economic and social constraints:

Strong kinship bonds among a variety of family households;
strong work, education, and achievement orientation;
high level of flexibility in family roles;
strong commitment to religious values and church participation; and
a humanistic orientation for perceiving the world and relationships.
(Springate and Stegelin 1999, 106)

Some students in America are biracial or multiracial. In this situation, you should determine the parents' desires about their child's heritage. Some parents of biracial children prefer to think of their children as "just children" and not as members of any race. Others acknowledge both backgrounds and have definite desires about how their children should be treated.

What can we do to foster collaboration with parents?

As we as teachers and caregivers work to build partnerships with families, we must do the following:

- Examine our own prejudices and preconceived ideas about how interested and capable families are on the basis of such factors as income, education, or ethnic background
- Ask parents what they need to assist them in nourishing the growth of their children, rather than make those decisions for them
- Be creative in developing strategies for involving families with diverse life situations, including dual-career families, single-parent families, families in

need of child care to attend meetings, families with limited transportation, and families who for some reason feel intimidated by the school environment
- Advocate for the time and economic human resources that are needed to implement programs involving families
- Make declarations in print, spoken words, and actions that address the school's commitment to involving families in the lives of the children at school. (Springate and Stegelin 1999, 53)

Whew! That's a tall order, particularly when some parents do *not* want to be involved! But we need help with our tough kids, and the best place to start is with their families.

How and When Do You Communicate with Parents?

What are your views toward those who are different?   Before you begin communicating with parents of tough kids, you must be aware about *your* views regarding the following:

- How do you view single parents?
- How do you view religious differences?
- How do you view same-gender partners as heads of household?
- How do you view poor families? Do you blame them for their poverty?
- How do you view different ethnic and racial groups? Are your views stereotypic?

Not too many years ago, a nearby major university demanded that freshmen state their religious affiliation on the registration form. Because one of my friends was a devout atheist and did not want to be "bedeviled by Bible thumpers," he wrote that he was a Buddhist. Imagine his surprise when a Buddhist priest who was originally from Tibet knocked on his door two weeks after school started! Imagine his mother's surprise when my friend became a Buddhist!

Because our school systems serve diverse ethnicities and religions, it is imperative that we examine our values and our beliefs about these differences. This does not mean that we scrap our value system and ascribe to those of others, but it does mean that we understand our beliefs, how our beliefs might cause us to judge others, and how these judgments might interfere with collaborating with parents. For example, an older married student in the education program at a nearby university divulged that she viewed single parenthood as "a sin and an abomination." Furthermore, she said that she would never allow her children to be taught by a single mother (unless she was a widow), nor would she tolerate an unmarried teacher who was living with a partner. Her student teaching was a nightmare for her as she struggled with children in a low-income neighborhood where many of the children had single mothers. Thankfully, when this teacher earned her teaching license, she chose to teach in a small religious school that reflected her values.

Your job is to listen to the parents so that you may help your students. This is going to be difficult if you feel that poor people could work if they wanted to, even if they have a two-hour commute on the bus, and even if child care chews up one-third of their salary. Or if you believe that all single moms should be married. Or you are nervous around those of a different race or religion.

The last year I taught in the classroom, my African American students thought that I was African American. How they determined that I was "light-skinned" is too complicated for this text, but my African American aide, who knew a good thing when she saw it, vowed to hurt me if I volunteered that I was "lily white." I never lied, mind you, and if my black students had asked me if I was white or black, I would have confessed, but they never asked. I had not realized the racial divide or the mistrust existing between parents and teachers until the final IEP (individualized education plan) conferences with my parents when I also told them that I would not be in the classroom the next year. Understandably, all the parents wanted to know who would teach their children with special needs the following year. One of my white parents, who thought that I was white, asked whether the teacher for their children the following year would be white or black. When I asked this parent why she wanted to know, she muttered, "You know how they are." I didn't, so this mother offered, "Well, *they* can be pretty rough with the kids. Don't want my child hurt." Interestingly, two of the black parents wanted to know the same thing, the race of their children's teacher the following year. When I again asked why this was important, one parent said, "Because I just don't want my child mistreated."

I had taught some of these children for four years, and I was hopelessly attached to them. They were my babies. I let both black and white parents understand that if anyone hurt my babies, I would hurt them. I would have.

And then I pondered how strange race and ethnicity is, and how often we don't understand the other fella.

What are the school guidelines for communicating with parents? Okay, you have all the information about your tough kids, including the scoop about the parents, and you have examined your values and possible prejudices. Now you need to understand the school guidelines for communicating with parents, particularly difficult parents. One of my parents threatened to shoot me and all the members of my class. This parent was warned off the property, and school administration forbade me to have written or verbal communication with this mother without the principal's approval, and the office handled all appointments for conferences. Many principals have definite guidelines about how to communicate with parents, even when the parents don't threaten homicide.

- Do written contacts with parents need principal approval?
- Should you have someone from the school accompany you on parent visits?
- What are the school's expectations for how many parents you should meet within a year? If you are teaching 150 students in high school, are you expected to conference with all of them sometime during the year?
- If the parents are divorced, do the records indicate who has custody, and with whom do you share the student's progress?
- If the records or teacher talk indicate that the child has a guardian, do you share information with the parents also?
- What should you do if a parent's expectations are unrealistic? For example, if they are:
   1) visiting or calling every day?
   2) contacting you by e-mail every day?
   3) demanding that they move their child to a higher academic group before the child is ready?

When should you contact parents, particularly parents of tough kids? Immediately! Yesterday! Don't wait until there's a problem!

If teacher talk and school records indicate that one or more of your students is considered a tough kid, contact the parents or guardians *before* school starts. If they have a phone either at home or at work, call them. Begin by apologizing for disturbing them (Whitaker and Fiore 2001). I usually contacted parents of my tough kids in the following manner:

"Mrs. Jones, I'm sorry to bother you at work (or at home). My name is Patty Pullen, and I'm going to be Suzie's teacher this year. I hope Suzie can have a good year, and wonder if you have any suggestions about how I can help her have a good year."

This shows that you're interested in Suzie, that you want parental involvement in Suzie's school year, and that you aren't dwelling on past misbehavior. Always look to the future! After a brief conversation, you might tell the parent that you will check with them again after school starts to make sure that Suzie isn't experiencing problems that you are not aware of. Also, give them your phone number so that they can contact you. But most importantly, listen to the parents!

One parent volunteered that her daughter had been a "mess" the previous year because she was flat-out bored. Apparently, the teacher had not determined her daughter's skill levels and had insisted on reteaching goals the student had mastered. This was a single mother who worked a job and a half, but she dropped by the school to show me the papers she had saved of her daughter's homework, class work, and test papers from "the year *before* hell." She also had the papers from the year of hell. I wanted to throttle the teacher from hell.

Another parent told me that she was tired of teachers' inability to control her son's behavior by always "pattin' him up." She also said, "If he gives you any trouble, knock him on his ass." This was valuable information. I kept this parent informed of her son's progress, but I did not involve her in any school behavior management plan. It's preferable not to involve the parents in a home/school plan if you think the following conditions occur:

- If you suspect abuse.
- If you suspect that the parent will not consistently implement the plan.

This is a situation when the social worker can help develop parenting skills, provide transportation for the parent to come to school, and help you develop a relationship with the parent.

If parents don't have a home phone and don't work, make a home visit. This advice is controversial, but I have had success visiting parents of tough kids before they come to school. It's best to follow these guidelines:

- Make sure that you have examined your prejudices and won't judge harshly when you go.
- Don't go alone. Try to find either someone the family knows to go with you, or someone who is familiar with the area.
- Apologize for disturbing them and ask if it would be better if you made an appointment to see them. (Sometimes the social worker can make an appointment for you.)
- If they ask you in, don't sit down unless they ask you to.
- Use the same message you would use if you had phoned them—you are looking to the future, want a good year for their child, and want suggestions from them.

Depending on the parents' reaction to your visit, you might ask how you can communicate with them in the future. I usually used what one of my parents called "the-back-and-forth-notebook."

What about letters home?   Introductory letters home before the students arrive can be valuable in establishing contact with parents. If you don't have many students, or if the school and/or you can afford the postage, send a letter home before the students come to school. If not, an introductory letter should be sent home with the students the first day of school. The letter should be brief, simply written, and give information about how to contact you, both at home and at work. For example:

Dear Parents,

My name is Patty Pullen, and I'll be your child's teacher this year.

Home phone: 555-1111

Work phone: 555-2222

I don't have a phone in my classroom, so I may have to call you back.

But I shall return your call as soon as I can. I'm looking forward to

meeting you. I need you!

Letters to parents of students that I had previously taught were more personal, and delineated some of the behavioral and academic goals with which we would begin the year. Sometimes I would include my behavior management plan or at least my classroom rules. But keep it simple, keep it friendly, and do it soon. And whatever the method of communicating with parents, the first contact should be positive. *Don't wait until there is a problem before contacting parents.*

What do I do if the parents become verbally abusive? I am grateful that in my long career in the classroom, I had very few parents that were abusive; when this did happen, it was unnerving to say the least, and sometimes downright frightening. The following are some guidelines for facing an angry parent:

- Remain calm.
- Do not make angry responses.
- Speak softly.
- If you are in error, admit it. (It's best to contact the parents with the error before they find out from their child.)
- Maintain eye contact.

Angry, abusive parents are often difficult because they may feel guilty about their child's lack of achievement, may feel overwhelmed by poverty, or may have had bad experiences with schools in the past. Whatever the reason, you don't want to be defensive or to argue. Remember, you need them! And also, you don't want to give them ammunition to take to your principal or the superintendent. Most importantly, you cannot win an argument with them, but may succeed in making them angrier. So don't hang up the phone or walk away if they become abusive. Don't scream or respond defensively or angrily. Some suggest that you handle abusive parents in the following manner: "Mrs. Smith, please don't talk to me that way. I will *never* speak to you like that, and I will *never* speak to your son/daughter like that" (Whitaker and Fiore 2001, 119).

Delivery is everything with this statement. You must be calm, speak softly, maintain eye contact, and not get into the back-and-forth of an argument that you can't win. This statement also requires that you know yourself, know that you really *never* would speak to anyone, particularly your students, the way the parent is speaking to you. You should also focus on the future, and try to steer the conversation to how you can prevent this problem from erupting again. And if you have made a mistake that has infuriated the parent, admit it, and share how you will prevent this from happening again.

A final important point is that parents are often most anxious with transitions; when their children have to change schools, such as going from elementary to middle school, parents' anxiety ratchets up. For example, a young mother of a Down syndrome five-year-old called me at home before teacher workdays. Mrs. Jones was very anxious about her son, Mark. In particular, she was nervous about the fact that my class had a reputation for integrating students in the regular classroom whenever possible. Mark had been in a nurturing preschool program for three years, and Mrs. Jones feared that Mark's kindergarten classmates might tease him or treat him like the class "mascot." I promised her that we would be attentive to Mark and that he would never be left alone, and she relaxed—a bit.

Imagine my surprise when I returned from a brief office visit the first day of class to find the student teacher who had been reading Mark a story in tears, the class snickering, and my aide trying not to laugh. And Mark was missing. According to my aide, Mark had asked to go to the bathroom, and after a few minutes, came out of the bathroom "buck naked." All of his clothes, including his shoes and socks, were in the toilet. My aide had put the buck-naked Mark behind a movable bulletin board in the corner of my room until she could scare up some clothes for him, and I had to call his mother!

I was horrified. I had promised this anxious mother that I would take care of her son, and there he sat naked as the day he was born with all his clothes in the toilet! I called the mother to ask her to bring more clothes to school (all we could find were a pair of rosebud underpants) and to apologize profusely. She was very southern, very gracious, and said that Mark had always wanted to put his clothes in the toilet and threatened to do so every day. She ended by saying, "Mrs. Pullen, you have fulfilled a lifelong dream for Mark!"

When Mrs. Jones arrived at school, Mark, a strapping, husky five-year-old, sat in my room—in his rosebud underpants. She said, "Why, Mark, why aren't you at lunch with your little friends?"

He responded in a husky voice while looking at his near-naked body, "No clothes."

"Why Mark, you don't have on any clothes! Where are your clothes?"

"In duh toilet."

I was trying hard not to laugh, but I just couldn't help myself. This broad little boy, in rosebud pants, the crying student teacher, my anxiety, this lovely mother—it was too much!

Mrs. Jones asked to speak to me in the hall. As I wiped my eyes, she said, "Now, Mrs. Pullen, we don't want to laugh at Mark because he might think it's funny that he put his clothes in the toilet and do it again! We don't want that, now, do we?"

I collapsed in laughter again—not the best thing to do, but I couldn't help it. Mrs. Jones started laughing too. She and I stood in the hall, holding onto each other and whooping. We learned two things about each other that day. She learned that I would always take responsibility for my mistakes. I learned that she was a forgiving parent who would always be there when I needed her. And after a few days, Mark learned that he could not go to the bathroom by himself until we were comfortable that he wouldn't put all his clothes in "duh toilet."

SUMMARY

Collaborating with the parents of our students is one of the most important aspects of teaching, but there aren't many guidelines for doing so, and often the prospect of relating to parents makes some of us downright nervous. Try to remember the following:

- Know your prejudices and how these prejudices will impact your interactions with parents.
- Know the school guidelines for dealing with parents.
- Always look to the future and how you can help the student. Don't dwell on past mistakes.
- Never argue with a parent. You can't win.
- If you mess up, learn from your mistakes and remember that you'll have another chance real soon to try again.

REFERENCES

Annie E. Casey Foundation. 2003. At www.accf.org/kidscount/databook/summary/summary12htm.

Connecticut Department of Social Services. 1999. At www.dss.state.ct.us.

Department of Social Services 2003. At www.dss.state.va.us.

National Center for Homeless Education. 1999. At www.serve.org/nche/SEAS-data.htm.

Springate, K. W., and D. A. Stegelin. 1999. *Building school and community partnerships through parent involvement.* Upper Saddle River, N.J.: Prentice Hall.

U.S. Bureau of the Census. 1999. At www.census.gov.

U.S. Bureau of Labor Statistics. 1997. At http://stats.bls.gov.

Walker, H. M., G. Colvin, and E. Ramsey. 1995. *Antisocial behavior in school: Strategies and best practices.* Pacific Grove, Calif.: Brooks/Cole.

Whitaker, T., and D. J. Fiore. 2001. *Dealing with difficult parents and with parents in difficult situations.* Larchmont, N.Y.: Eye on Education.

4

BEHAVIOR
MODIFICATION

A relative tells the story about an acquaintance who was paddling through the bayous of Louisiana on a scientific expedition. There were several boats in this expedition, and it was the job of the occupants in the lead boat to knock the water moccasins from the low overhang into the water so that the snakes would not drop into the boats or onto the people as they passed underneath. The "knocker" missed a snake, which fell into the bottom of the acquaintance's boat. In a panic, this scientist yelled, "I got it! I got it!" He grabbed a shotgun and shot the snake. The snake died. The boat sank.

Sometimes we shoot the boats right out from under us when we don't have adequate behavior management plans. I cannot provide a course in behavior management in this chapter, but I can give you guidelines with the hope that you won't shoot holes in your boat.

If "teacher talk," school records, and parent contact indicate you have a tough kid or two, what proactive techniques can you use to prevent misbehavior?

BEFORE YOU BEGIN: LOOK AT INSTRUCTION

"Behavior problems are not always a result of poor choices of curriculum or teaching strategies, but these must be the first factors we examine" (Kauffman, Mostert, Trent, and Hallahan 2002, 6). Geoffrey Colvin of the University of

Oregon states in his video on behavior management, "The oldest variable in the book in terms of proactive strategies is good teaching—quality instruction" (Colvin 1992).

But what is *good teaching?* What is *quality instruction?* The answers to the preceding questions are as varied and as controversial as any issue in education.

Characteristics of Best Instructional Practices

Some authors refer to the following as the keys to offering effective instruction:

1. *Clarity*—The student must know exactly what to do (i.e., have no doubt about what is expected).
2. *Level*—The student must be able to do the task with a high degree of accuracy (i.e., be able to get *at least* 80 percent correct), but the task must be challenging (i.e., the student should not easily get 100 percent correct repeatedly).
3. *Opportunities*—The student must have frequent opportunities to respond (i.e., be actively engaged in the task a high percentage of the time).
4. *Consequence*—The student must receive a meaningful reward for correct performance (i.e., the consequences of correct performance must be frequent and perceived as desirable by the student).
5. *Sequence*—The tasks must be presented in logical sequence so that the student gets the big idea (i.e., steps must be presented and learned in order so that the knowledge or skill is built on a logical progression or framework of ideas, which is a systematic curriculum).
6. *Relevance*—The task must be relevant to the student's life so that, if possible, the student understands how and why it is useful (i.e., the teacher attempts to help the student see why in his or her culture the task is important).
7. *Application*—The teacher must help the student learn how to learn and remember by teaching memory and learning strategies and applying knowledge and skills to everyday problems (i.e., the teacher teaches generalizations, not just isolated skills, and honors the student's culture).
8. *Monitoring*—The teacher must continuously monitor student progress (i.e., record and chart progress, always know and be able to show what the student has mastered and the student's place or level in a curriculum or sequence of tasks). (Kauffman et al. 2002, 7)

The preceding assumes that you have determined the skill levels of your tough kids from the school records and teacher talk. If you don't know where your students are in their skills, you won't know whether the *level* of difficulty is appropriate, regardless of the *clarity* of the instruction. And even if you provide ample *opportunities* to practice the skills, the students may not take advantage of these opportunities if they haven't mastered the skills. And if you don't know a student's level, you can forget *application.* If the students are bored because the skills have been in their repertoire for a long time, or if they are nervous because they don't know the skill you wish them to apply, they will probably not even try. They will occupy themselves with other endeavors—things like writing notes, picking their noses, teasing classmates, or having tantrums. That won't float your boat.

Before you can adapt the curriculum for your tough kids, determine how delayed they are, and who could help you adapt the curriculum. This requires that you consult the information gleaned from the folders and the teacher talk. You may need to consult another teacher and ask specific questions.

How delayed are my tough kids?

• Is he or she a year or more behind classmates in particular skills?
• Is he or she a nonreader?
• Does he or she receive services from special education?
    1) If so, what are the services and how intensive are they? (e.g., how many hours per day?)
    2) Who provides the services?
• Do the records indicate that there was a recent referral, but that an evaluation has not been completed?
• Do records indicate major revisions in the curriculum? Or were minor adjustments successful?
• Is it unclear whether any curriculum adaptations were made?
• Does the information from records and teachers indicate that the student is more delayed in one subject?

If you discover that a tough kid of yours is delayed academically but there are no records of how the curriculum was adapted for the student, you need some help.

Who can help? First, look for professionals whose names appear in the student's records: previous teachers, special education staff, or guidance counselors. Sometimes parents will tell you that Johnny got better grades in Mrs. X's class. Find Mrs. X, who may have made curriculum modifications that are not in the records.

You may have a list of names of staff whom you contacted when reading the records, folks who have already given you valuable information. Contact them again if you need to.

But *never* forget that the best behavior management tool is good teaching! "Contrary to popular belief, many off-task and disruptive behaviors in classrooms are probably not maintained by teacher attention. Instead, students often use these behaviors to escape or avoid an instructional task" (Cipani 1995, 36). They do.

Behavior Considerations

Your tough kids fit the category of folks my grandmother labeled as being so contrary that they would argue with a fence post. Indeed. These are the students who make teachers and other students edgy, frustrated, and angry. They use noncompliance to suck teachers into arguments that we can't win. Their mantra seems to be, "I'm not going to do it, and you can't make me!" Unfortunately, many of us persist in arguing with our tough kids, placing more sanctions on their noncompliance until somebody wins—usually the tough kid. They are very good at their "kingpin" job and do not easily relinquish this power. Why should they? The short-term payoffs for them are huge. They get out of doing work. They control their classmates and teachers. They derive great joy from pushing our buttons and watching us blast off. Other tough kids learn from them and become tougher.

A few easily implemented strategies will help keep the lid on the tough kids' eruptions.

- Do you have rules that you enforce?
- Do you know what your tough kids will work for?
- Do you use crisis prevention strategy for really tough kids?
- Do you have assigned seats and other structures built into the day?
- Do you have a fast-paced schedule with little or no downtime?

What about rules? Rules are a vital part of classroom structure in all grades. But there are some rules about rules.

- Don't pile on the rules. Try to keep the list short. Don't have more than five rules, and because compliance is a hurdle for tough kids, always have a compliance rule first. The following is an example of rules that an elementary school teacher might use:
  1) Do what teachers ask immediately.
  2) Keep your hands and feet and everything to yourself.
  3) Raise your hand and wait to be called on before talking unless we have free time.
- Be careful how you word your rules. Rules should have the following characteristics:
  1) Keep the wording positive when possible (i.e., say what to do, not what not to do).
  2) Keep your rules specific. No ambiguity. Students need to know exactly what is expected.
  3) Make your rules describe behavior that is observable and measurable. Rules that describe feelings or other internal states, or that require subjective judgments, are full of ambiguity and will cause you trouble.
  4) Tie following the rules to the consequences. What good thing will happen if students follow the rules, and also what mild punishments will result from not following the rules?
  5) Post rules and consequences so that you can refer to them. (Rhode, Jenson, and Reavis 1993, 22)
- Rules that are not specific, observable, or measurable are not good rules. In the following rules, the words "respect," "good citizen," or "best" can have wide interpretation among students and teachers:
  1) Be responsible.
  2) Be a good citizen.
  3) Demonstrate respect for others.
  4) Respect others' rights.
  5) Do your best. (Rhode et al. 1993, 22)
     The preceding are concepts that you want to teach, or discuss with your class; however, they don't make good rules.

- Have a hierarchy of positive and negative consequences posted beside the rules. The following is an example:

IF YOU FOLLOW THE RULES, YOU CAN EARN THE FOLLOWING:	IF YOU DON'T FOLLOW THE RULES:
1. Extra free time.	1. Loss of extra free time.
2. A turn at the class "grab bag."	2. Get a phone call to your parents.
3. Lottery tickets for mystery prize.	3. Go to in-school suspension.
4. Lunch with the teacher [or for older children, homework pass].	4. Lose school privileges (for example, lunch with your friends).

What is positive reinforcement and how do you use it? The preceding chart assumes that the reinforcers listed are desirable for the students. One of the main reasons for meeting with other teachers is to determine what a particular tough kid has worked for in the past, and also what that student considers mild punishment.

The definition of positive reinforcement is that it increases the likelihood of the desired behavior when it is given contingent upon that behavior. So it's important for you to determine what teachers have used successfully to motivate a tough kid. And it's also important for you to remember what some researchers determine is the golden rule for selecting reinforcers. "The Golden Rule states that any selected reinforcers should not cost a lot of money, should not take a lot of staff time, and should be natural, whenever possible" (Rhode et al. 1993, 40).

Natural reinforcers are those that occur naturally in the environment, and ones that you don't have to pay for. Usually, these are things like helping out, which many kids consider privileges. For example, one school where I taught did not have a cafeteria. All the children ate in their classrooms from plastic containers. Each classroom had a huge barrel with a heavy plastic bag where the students dumped the trays, and after lunch the custodian collected the plastic bags, tied them up, and carried them to the school dumpsters. The fifth-grade boys worked hard for the privilege of helping the custodian gather up the bags of lunch trash. Most of us would not find this privilege reinforcing, but the boys did. Even the custodian was a bit confused by this arrangement. Why would kids want to do this? But they did, and that's what mattered.

The teacher of a summer school program for gifted middle school students was also puzzled by her students' choice of positive reinforcement. One of these gifted students sauntered into the library one morning when the librarian was ripping the covers off outdated magazines that she was going to throw away. The student asked the librarian if he could have one of these ripped magazines, and she replied, "Well, I'm not just going to give this to you. But maybe you would like to work for it." He did! And he also persuaded his classmates to do the same.

When I was at the beach one year, a storm deposited lots of seashells on the beach. Most of the shells were tiny, but I thought these shells would be great positive reinforcers for my class. They were. For students learning a new skill, I gave a small shell for each correct written response. Later, I faded the reinforcement to three correct responses per shell, then five, then ten, and then none. The students loved the shells, worked hard for them, and I paid not one nickel for them.

Extra free time, extra time on the computer, free time with a friend, or lunch with a favorite teacher are examples of naturally occurring reinforcers. Because tough kids need *lots* of reinforcement, and because they need to learn to postpone gratification, you need to build in small reinforcements, not huge ones. The general rule for positive reinforcement is to make it small and frequent, not huge and seldom. For example, in the preceding vignette about gifted students who worked for tattered magazines, their teachers awarded them points during the morning for specific behaviors. When the students accrued the predetermined number of points on a chart, they could go to the library and pick out a torn-up magazine.

Some other cautions about positive reinforcement: It takes longer to work than punishment, it won't work if the student doesn't find the reward reinforcing, and if you are inconsistent in administering the reward, the student won't work for the reward. So make sure of the following:

1. The student wants the reward.
2. You administer the reinforcement *often* when the skill is new.
3. You are scrupulously *consistent* in giving the reward.

One of my student teachers was incensed that I gave my students rewards for academic and social success. She thought that these students should do the work and behave *because they were supposed to.* "They should do what I tell them to do without my having to reward them!" Maybe they should. But the reality is that many won't. And complaining in the face of this reality is one way to shoot a hole in your boat. Many tough kids are from chaotic families who have also failed in the school system, and even though these parents love their children, many don't monitor homework or ask to see class work or test papers; which means that the parents don't see the work and therefore don't say what most of us say to our children, "That's a great paper! Good for you!"

So give your tough kids contingent and noncontingent reinforcement:

1. Contingent reinforcement: The reward is contingent on the student performing a specific task or skill.
2. Noncontingent reinforcement: The attention we give students because they are human beings and therefore deserve this attention, such as telling them you like their new hairdo, asking them to pass out materials for you, asking them to run an errand for you, or just talking with them. Too often, teachers let tough kids become so awful that they then don't want any interaction with them. A tough kid needs attention, encouragement, and rewarding relationships with adults.

Some teachers refer to rewarding students as bribing them. The definition of a bribe is an inducement given for corrupt behavior. We don't ask our tough kids to do anything corrupt for their rewards, and we give them something they probably don't get anywhere else—attention for performing academically and socially. Ask yourself this: Is the school board bribing me to teach by sending me a paycheck every month?

Always pair any tangible reinforcement with social reinforcement, such as description of the skill you're reinforcing accompanied by praise, a wink, or a pat on the back. Eventually, for most kids, you can maintain skills with social reinforcement, which is the ultimate goal for our tough kids. But be advised: some of our difficult students will need reinforcement throughout their academic careers. The tougher the kids, the more reinforcement they usually need. Remember that your classroom demands may be competing with years of entrenched misbehavior that has provided *big* payoffs—lots of attention from peers and adults for being bad. Unfortunately, you have to compete with those payoffs.

The following is a final plea for why teachers should use lots of positive reinforcement:

- The majority of these tough kids have a long history of punishment to which they have grown immune.
- They have a high risk for school dropout (estimated to be 65 percent) and will not stay in nonpositive environments.
- In the long run, permanent behavior changes are maintained only by basic positive procedures. (Rhode et al. 1993, 2)

What procedures do you have in place for the really toughies? Some of your students may be hyperaggressive. If teacher talk and student records suggest that you have a student who has tantrums or violent and aggressive behavior, you need to plan for this unpleasant eventuality. Discuss with your administrators what support you can expect if this student becomes violent in your classroom. Specifically, who will you contact for help, and how will you communicate your need? Some teachers prepare a laminated card with a signal on it (one teacher drew a blazing campfire) that they send to the office when a hyperaggressive student becomes violent. Don't try to handle or restrain a violent student by yourself.

What is crisis prevention strategy? Difficult students derive joy and usually get out of doing work by drawing us into an argument. They are *so* good at what many term engaging behavior—drawing us into a battle. They do this very simply by taking turns. The teacher makes a request (the teacher's turn) and the student responds (the student's turn). For example,

the following is an interaction between an eighth-grade math teacher and a
difficult student who is trying to engage her:

> Teacher (standing at the door as students enter): Please have a seat and do the
> warm-up assignment on the board.
> Johnny (standing in the doorway): Not that again! I'm not doin' that stupid ol'
> stuff anymore!
> Teacher: Please come in and take your seat, Johnny.
> Johnny: I don't think so, Teach'! Don't think you're woman enough to make
> me either.
> Teacher: Please come and sit down.
> Johnny: Now, calm down, Teach'.
> Teacher: Please use my name when you speak to me.
> Johnny: Okay, Teach', I mean, Ms. Pullen.
> Teacher: Please move out of the doorway so the other students can come in!
> Johnny: Now Teach'. You're gettin' all worked up.
> Teacher: Move now!
> Johnny: Who you yellin' at? I don't have to do what you say.
> Teacher: Oh, yes you do! Come in and sit down!
> Johnny: Well, maybe you can make me, Bitch!
> Teacher: No, but I can write a referral for calling me a name!
> Johnny: Go ahead! I don't give a damn!
> Teacher: Go to the office!
> Johnny: Nope. Think I'll go take my seat now.
> Teacher: No, you will go immediately to the office as I have instructed you to do!
> When Johnny tries to push past the teacher, she grabs his arm. He hits her.

The preceding illustrates the interactions between a teacher and a student
who successfully engages the teacher—a series of "my turn–your turn" interactions that culminates in a teacher getting hit and a student probably getting
suspended. When you use crisis prevention strategies, *don't take your turn.*
Let's look at this interaction again when the teacher uses crisis prevention
strategies.

> Teacher (standing at the doorway as students enter): Please have a seat and do
> the warm-up assignment on the board.
> Johnny (standing in the doorway): Not that again! I'm not doin' that stupid ol'
> stuff anymore!

Teacher: Please come in and take your seat, Johnny.

Johnny: I don't think so, Teach'. Don't think you're woman enough to make me either.

Teacher (lowers her voice, is very calm): Come in now and sit down, or I'll call your parents. You have a few seconds to decide.

(The teacher begins to chat with another student sitting close to the door. She does not look at Johnny for a few seconds. After a few seconds, she approaches Johnny.)

Teacher: Johnny, come and sit down, please.

Johnny shuffles into the room, bangs his backpack onto the desk, and sits down.

Teacher (approaches Johnny): Thanks.

The following are guidelines for using crisis prevention strategies:

- Have a "bottom line" consequence that you and an administrator have decided on before the crisis develops. (You don't have to inform the student what this bottom line is beforehand.) The consequence could be a visit to the principal's office, calling parents, calling the police, or removing a desired free-time activity.
- Issue this consequence *very calmly as a choice.* "Either you sit down or I'll call your parents."
- State the consequence and choice in *one* sentence followed by the statement, "You have a few seconds to decide."
- Move away immediately from the tough kid. Give him or her some space to make the decision.
- After a few seconds, come back to the student and present the choice again.
- *Follow through with consequences:* either thank the student for complying or implement the punishment. Once you state that punishment is going to happen, do not be dissuaded by late compliance. Some students will move quickly to comply once you begin to implement the punishment. It's too late then! For example, in the preceding vignette, if the teacher buzzes the office on the intercom, and asks the principal to call Johnny's parents, and Johnny suddenly sits down, it's too late. The principal must still call the parents.
- Remain calm and respectful.

- Debrief later when the student is calm and responsive to your questions.
  1) What was your behavior?
  2) What was your concern or need?
  3) What else could you have done that would have been acceptable and would have met your need?
  4) What will you do next time if this situation arises? (Colvin 1992)

What *not* to do when implementing crisis prevention strategies:

- Don't fuss at the student, touch, or make demeaning remarks about him or her.
- Don't stand over the student or stare at him or her after you issue the "either/or" order.
- Don't use a lot of words. More than a sentence or two gives the student an opportunity to engage you.
- Don't give a specific time limit (e.g., ten seconds) for complying.
- *Don't take your turn.* Even if the student fusses or uses foul language while you give them a few seconds to decide, don't take your turn.

Tough kids often can't handle a lot of choices, so an either/or statement works best for them. When I have observed teachers implementing this strategy, the most-often-repeated mistakes are using too many words and giving a specific time to comply. The following is an example of doing it wrong:

"Johnny, I know that you are upset, and I want to hear about what has upset you, but not now. You and I have never had a problem so let's not start now. Either sit down and get quiet or I'll call your parents. You have ten seconds to decide."

In the preceding incident, the teacher's words were kind and understanding, but there were too many of them. Every word was an opportunity for the student to engage the teacher, and the important message—either sit down or I'll call your parents—was muddied by all the verbiage. But the crowning blow to this teacher was that the class began counting down the time—"ten, nine, eight, seven, six, five, four, three, two, one." The teacher achieved blast off.

Another mistake teachers often make when implementing crisis prevention strategies is to allow the student to comply inappropriately. For example, in the preceding dialogue, if the student refuses to sit down, then the teacher buzzes the office to ask for help. After the teacher pushes the intercom button, Johnny runs to his seat, sits down, and says, "Hey, I'm sittin' down now, Teach'. Look at me, I'm sittin' down." That's too late, and if the teacher relents, Johnny has learned that he never has to comply when you ask him to. He knows that he can create a chaotic situation whenever he wants. It's the wrong kind of control to give a tough kid.

Tough kids want control, and we give them appropriate control when we use crisis prevention strategies correctly. They make the choice. We're out of the controversy because we don't take our turn. They save face. We don't get a migraine.

When do you step in? Because many teachers don't have a clue what behaviors lead to violent or aggressive behavior, we often allow a child to spin out of control when we could halt the process with crisis prevention or some other form of mild punishment. For example, I made the mistake of being ill for two weeks one year, and an eight-year-old hyperaggressive student in my class took advantage of my absence. After a week, he decided that he wasn't coming to school until I returned. One morning, his mother wrestled him into the car, and the principal carried him into my classroom. (The mother beat a hasty retreat.) "Anthony" refused to sit down. He paced and expounded on what he would do to his mother when he got home. My aide decided not to engage him and let him rant. His threats became louder and after a few minutes, he began to direct these threats at his classmates and the aide. When he stood in front of another student and asked, "Do you want the rescue squad to pick you up after I get through with you?" the aide intervened. Anthony hit the aide and the other student. The principal sent him home and suspended him for a day.

In the preceding situation, the aide should have intervened immediately when Anthony refused to sit down and was threatening others. Instead, she chose to ignore the behavior, which escalated to unmanageable proportions. There are specific guidelines for ignoring unwanted behavior. They are the following:

1. The behavior you ignore will get worse before it gets better.
2. Ignoring behavior will only work if the behavior is for teacher attention.

3. Have a replacement behavior that you reinforce that is incompatible with the unwanted behavior.
4. *Never ignore the first stages of violent or aggressive behavior.*

Impose sanctions immediately when students show the slightest hint of violent behavior. In this situation, the second Anthony refused to sit down and be quiet, the aide should have said, "Anthony, either sit down and be quiet, or I'll call security. You have a few seconds to decide." Then the aide should have moved away and let him decide.

Teachers often complain that some administrators are too tough on kids who are just being kids. Behavior such as students playfully shoving each other, students chasing each other around the classroom, or yelling provocative comments are often tolerated because "kids will be kids." But a tough kid will escalate into a crisis before you can blink, which means that you don't tolerate any aggressive behavior in your classroom, even if the kids are "just playing."

The rules are helpful in situations similar to Anthony's episode. For example, the following is a possible scenario:

Aide: Anthony, sit down and be quiet now, please.
Anthony: Do you want the rescue squad to pick up what's left of you in a minute?
Aide (pointing to the rule): Are you doing what I ask? Either sit down and be quiet as I asked, or lose your extra free time.

Later, when Anthony is quiet and calm, you would debrief.

Or if students began to engage in horseplay, shoving and pushing each other, you refer to the rules, which may include "Keep your hands and feet and everything to yourself," and ask, "Are you keeping your hands and feet and everything to yourself? Stop now or lose some of your extra free time." Later, as the students became familiar with the rules, inform them that you will subtract time from their extra free time without a warning. "You're not keeping your hands and feet and everything to yourself. You lose two minutes of your extra time."

Delivery is everything when you intervene with tough kids. They derive great pleasure in pushing our buttons and watching us explode. So adhere to the following:

- Show no anger.
- The reprimand must be as private as possible.
- Keep voice low and calm. Show no affect—no angry frowns or "I got you" smirks.
- Keep your body still and in neutral—no hands on your hips. Keep your hands still and in sight of the student.
- Implement the consequence *immediately*. If the sanction is loss of free time, then subtract minutes from free time as soon as you see students exhibiting potentially violent behavior.

When do you refer a student to child study? Even though many preach that early intervention is the key to preventing antisocial behavior from becoming entrenched, there is still the prevailing fallacy that a young child will "outgrow" the problem. Not so, and this popular belief guarantees that many children are on a fast train to behavior disorders.

"Ironically, the most powerful evidence in support of the prevention of delinquency comes from long-term, follow-up studies of childhood programs targeting at-risk children very early in their school careers. These intervention programs were designed not to prevent delinquency, but rather to prevent the school failure of at-risk populations" (Walker, Ramsey, and Gresham 2004, 57).

If you are an early childhood teacher, document the tough kid's academic and behavioral deficits and refer the student to child-study committee. It has been my experience that most of the kindergarten children who were referred were not identified as students with special needs; however, many of the children who were identified in later grades as special education students were originally brought to the child-study team in kindergarten.

Teachers in all the other grades do the same thing. Record a tough kid's deficits, and ask for help. The tough kid deserves the help, and you need the support.

Why use behavior management? Use behavior management as a way to gain rapport with a tough kid. Joshua is an example of the pluses of gaining and keeping rapport with a tough kid. Joshua enrolled in my class on February 14, and he was no Valentine. After a few days, my aide said, "Pullen, I think you've met your match." I thought so too, but after two weeks, Joshua settled into the routine, and much to our amazement, Joshua became a compliant, hardworking student. I taught Joshua for three years, and he was one of my favorite students until my last week of school in my last year in the classroom when Joshua reverted to his Valentine's Day behavior. He was such a mess that teachers and other students wondered what had happened to him.

One of the established routines in my classroom was the "afternoon review" when the students and I sat around a large table, and they corrected the morning seatwork and homework. When all the seatwork and homework were completed, the students could have quiet free time. Joshua was not nice. He constantly muttered, wrote on his paper, and then immediately erased the answer. His usually immaculate papers were a mess of incorrect corrections. He glared provocatively at the other students who kept asking, "Ms. Pullen, what's wrong with Joshua?" Quite frankly, he was getting on my nerves.

"Please stop talking, Joshua."

He didn't.

"Joshua, please tell me why you're so angry."

He frowned and after a few moments said, "Ms. Pullen, you got no business quittin' teachin'!"

I said, "But Joshua, I would not be your teacher next year even if I continued to teach. You're going to middle school."

Joshua kept muttering, slamming his paper on the table, rubbing holes in his work with the eraser.

Finally he said, "You just don't get it, do you?"

I had had it. I said a bit louder than I should have, "No! But you're going to in a minute."

Joshua was very quiet for a few seconds and then he said, "Ms. Pullen, what about all them other little kids that are comin' up? What about them? Who's going to help them?"

And then he listed his misbehaviors in accurate detail—the nightmare behaviors that he exhibited when he walked into my classroom. I was astonished that he not only knew what he was doing that was wrong when he came to my class, but also that he credited my reinforcement and mild punishment with bringing about "this good change in me."

One by one, each child related his or her behavior when they came to the special education class, and how they had improved. Just like Joshua, every student enumerated his or her academic and behavioral deficits, and how the rules had helped.

One little girl said, "I hated you at first—how you never let me get by with *nothin'*. But you also showed me how good I could be."

When my aide returned from lunch, we were sitting at the table, passing around the box of tissues. She asked, "Who died while I was at lunch?"

This was a class of kindergarten through fourth grade students with mild mental handicaps. Even so, all of them understood that the rules, the sanctions, and the rewards helped them. My babies understood that behavior management was a tool to help them become better—to help them make a "good change." It is.

SUMMARY

- The best behavior management tool is *good teaching*.
- Post rules along with consequences.
- Implement the rules.
- Know what positive reinforcement is and why it is important.
- Use crisis prevention strategy.

REFERENCES

Cipani, E. C. 1995. Be aware of negative reinforcement. *Teaching Exceptional Children* 27, no. 4:36–40.

Colvin, G. 1992. *Managing acting-out behavior* (video program). Eugene, Ore.: Behavior Associates.

Kauffman, J. M., M. P. Mostert, S. C. Trent, and D. P. Hallahan. 2002. *Managing classroom behavior: A reflective case-based approach.* Boston, Mass.: Allyn and Bacon.

Rhode, G., W. R. Jenson, and K. R. Reavis. 1993. *The tough kid book: Practical classroom management strategies.* Longmont, Colo.: Sopris West.

Walker, H. M., E. Ramsey, and F. M. Gresham. 2004. *Antisocial behavior in school: Strategies and practices.* 2nd ed. Pacific Grove, Calif.: Brooks/Cole.

INDEX

ABOUT THE AUTHOR

Patty Pullen is an adjunct professor of licensure and graduate programs for special education teachers at the University of Virginia. She has spent most of her adult life teaching children and teaching adults how to teach children. She resides in Charlottesville, Virginia, with her husband.